W9-ACZ-134

DISCARD

Date: 3/20/18

J 152.4 DIN
Dinmont, Kerry,
Dan's first day of school : a
book about emotions /

PALM BEACH COUNTY
LIBRARY SYSTEM
3650 SUMMIT BLVD.
WEST PALM BEACH, FL 33406

Dan's First Day of School

A Book about Emotions

by Kerry Dinmont

Published by The Child's World®
1980 Lookout Drive • Mankato, MN 56003-1705
800-599-READ • www.childsworld.com

Photographs ©: ESB Professional/Shutterstock Images, cover, 3, 4, 6; Denis
Nata/Shutterstock Images, 8; Michael Jung/Shutterstock Images, 10; Jan
H. Andersen/Shutterstock Images, 12–13; iStockphoto, 15; Tomsickova
Tatyana/Shutterstock Images, 16–17; Shutterstock Images, 19; Thomas M.
Perkins/Shutterstock Images, 20

Copyright © 2018 by The Child's World®
All rights reserved. No part of this book may be reproduced or utilized in
any form or by any means without written permission from the publisher.

ISBN 9781503820197
LCCN 2016960944

Printed in the United States of America
PA02340

It is Dan's first day of school.

How does he feel?

Dan is excited. He will make new friends!

Mia is surprised. There are a lot of kids at school!

Liam is sad. He misses his family.

Matt is **proud**. He painted a picture in art class.

Ava is worried. She does not know where to sit in the lunchroom.

Lucas is happy.
He found
someone to play
with at recess!

Sofia is **content**. She likes her teacher.

How do you feel on the first day of school?

Glossary

content (kuhn-TENT) To feel content means to feel happy and peaceful. Sofia felt content after she met her nice teacher.

proud (PROWD) To feel proud means to feel happy and satisfied with what you have done. Matt was proud of his picture.

Extended Learning Activities

1. Think of a time you felt one of the emotions in this book. Where were you? What made you feel this way?

2. Who were some of the characters in this book?

3. What words in this book are words that describe emotions?

To Learn More

Books

Schiller, Abbie. *A Little Book about Feelings.*
2nd ed. Los Angeles, CA: Mother Co., 2012.

Witek, Jo. *In My Heart: A Book of Feelings.*
New York, NY: Abrams Appleseed, 2014.

Web Sites

Visit our Web site for links about emotions:
childsworld.com/links

Note to Parents, Teachers, and Librarians: We routinely verify our Web links to make sure
they are safe and active sites. So encourage your readers to check them out!

About the Author

Kerry Dinmont is a children's book author who enjoys
art and nature. She lives in Montana with her two
Norwegian elkhounds.